C000094656

Absence and Loss

Holocaust Memorials in Berlin and Beyond

Marion Davies

DAVID
PAUL

Published in Great Britain in 2007

By David Paul
25 Methuen Park
London N10 2JR

info@davidpaulbooks.com

www.davidpaulbooks.com

Distribution by Central Books, 99 Wallis Road, London E9 5LN

Photographs and captions © Marion Davies 2007
Texts: © the contributors 2007

Marion Davies has asserted her right to be to be identified as author of this book in accordance with the Copyright, Designs and Patents Act 1988

Design by David English

A CIP catalogue of this book is available from the British Library

ISBN 10 0-9548482-4-1
ISBN 13 978-0-9548482-4-8

Printed in Great Britain by Chandlers Printers Ltd, Bexhill-on-Sea

Contents

Acknowledgements   4

Foreword
Dr James Smith   5

The Art of Commemoration - Holocaust Memorials and their Makers
Julia Weiner   6

Holocaust Memorials of Berlin
Marion Davies   10

Absence and Loss: Holocaust Memorials in Berlin and Beyond   11

References   64

Acknowledgements

This book is the result of a long journey of exploration into the world my parents were forced to leave behind. It would not have come to fruition without the help of many people, in particular my husband Jonathan, who could not have imagined that his wife, a social worker, would take on a new life as a photographer. It has led us to many adventures and encounters. I thank him for his support during this project, for his patience and love and for carrying that heavy tripod. My children, Rachel, Simon and Jo, have adapted to a somewhat preoccupied mother and learned to avoid strips of negatives drying in the kitchen. They too are a terrific loving support and I want to thank them for their helpful contributions.

My parents can no longer appreciate the path I have gone down, but I am extremely grateful to them for my happy, cultured, Jewish upbringing. I would also like to acknowledge my dear friend Linda, who is very much missed. I know she would have supported me all the way.

Rachel first introduced me to her tutor, Margie Tolstoy, at Cambridge University. Her faith in my work resulted in an invitation to exhibit in Michaelhouse, Cambridge for Holocaust Memorial Day 2006. This was the first of several exhibitions and I am deeply grateful for the opportunity offered and the encouragement of both Margie and the Michaelhouse Chaplain, The Revd. Dr Andreas Loewe. The exhibition was based on a final module for a photographic BTEC at City of Westminster College and I would like to thank my tutors at the College for their input during the early stages. Thanks also go to Yakir Zur and Geoff and Jilly Davies who helped to promote the first exhibition and greatly eased my burden.

I would not like to forget those friends and family who helped put up and take down the exhibitions – also the many who have listened patiently, on walks and at other times, to my dilemmas and had constructive ideas. They have taken the time to read the text and made many helpful suggestions. In particular, I would like to thank Sir Martin Gilbert for generously making the time in his busy schedule to read the text on two occasions and for his helpful comments.

A special thank you to those whose portraits I have included in the book. To trust a stranger to take photos and to share a poignant part of their lives with her is something I find very humbling.

The book would not have been possible without the help of my publisher, David Paul, who has offered much more support and help than I ever imagined, and David English, the designer, who calmly listened to our plans and then created a far superior design.

I am also grateful to Dr James Smith for his thoughtful introduction and to Julia Weiner for her wise words on memorialisation, art and the Holocaust. They have added a quality to the work and to our understanding of the Holocaust and its consequences for us all today.

I am grateful to Memery Crystal and a private charitable trust for their generous support for the book and also to Werksmans, who have kindly agreed to sponsor the exhibition in Johannesburg.

Foreword

Dr James Smith

A picture tells a thousand words, or so it is said. Marion Davies's work supports that truism. It was with great pleasure that the Holocaust Centre was able to host last year an exhibition of her remarkable photographic essay on Germany's dialogue with the loss and absence of its once-thriving Jewish community, reproduced in the following pages.

The Centre regularly hosts exhibitions by artists addressing the Holocaust, but this was in some way different, not portraying directly the horror and pain of its victims but rather the footprints they left in the landscape of Germany, a country which – more than almost anywhere else in the world – the native Jewish community had embraced as its own. It is also about contemporary German society's interaction with the marks left by that community – in terms of architecture, sculpture and memorial.

It's a body of work that doesn't immediately scream at the viewer's emotions but – often like its subject matter – blends into the background, waiting to be noticed and explored. And then, when you dip in, you find yourself lost in a destroyed world, often discovering some new and poignant fact that you had not known before, and realising afresh that genocide does not end when the last victim is killed – its legacy goes on and will continue for generations.

But how do you engage with that legacy? Are architecture and memorial enough? Work such as the Berlin Jewish Museum's *Holocaust Tower* (page 11) or the cemetery-like *Memorial to the Murdered Jews of Europe* (page 63) encourage viewers to step aside from the rush of their lives and reflect. Their abstract nature is discomforting and illustrates the impossibility of art ever capturing the subject matter to which it speaks.

For me, however, the most powerful memorials are those which link to a specific time, place, group of people, or even just one individual. The re-erection of Mendelssohn's tombstone amid empty space where 3,000 Jewish gravestones once stood (page 15) is silent testament to the Nazi attempt to wipe out not only a people, but even the memory that they ever existed.

How do people react to that memory today? Information on photographs such as those of the memorial at Pulitzstrasse Station (page 47) and the mirrored wall at Steglitz market (page 50) show that the desire to forget, whether expressed subtly or crudely,

remains. Truth – particularly about such a horrible legacy – hurts. 'Men occasionally stumble over the truth, but most of them pick themselves up and hurry off as if nothing ever happened,' Winston Churchill famously once said.

Encouragingly, we also find people going out of their way to uncover and point to the memory of victims of the Holocaust who once inhabited their environments. The *Missing House Memorial* is enormously evocative (page 43), as is the brilliantly named *Stolpersteine*, (Stumblestone) project (page 23), initiated by the artist Gumner Demnig. This project engages the public, particularly young people, in researching their area's wartime past and commemorating local Jewish people killed in the Holocaust with bronze plaques embedded in the pavement at sites which relate to their lives and untimely deaths.

Overall, Marion Davies's work suggests that Germany is engaged in a very healthy, ongoing examination of its history. This impression is borne out in my experience of dealing with scholars and students from the country as they struggle with the legacy of the actions of their parents' and grandparents' generations, and seek inspiration from the small number who did have the courage to stand up to impossible odds to try to rescue their Jewish neighbours.

Denial of memory is the final act of genocide. If you can forget the past, repeating the atrocities becomes more possible. Germany has become a model for nations needing to embrace a dreadful heritage. Turkey should be inspired to address the destruction of the Armenians, Japan the rape of Nanjing. Acknowledging the deliberate loss of human life may be painful but, like opening a festering wound, allows it to heal.

It is fitting that this book is published in the year of the fiftieth anniversary of the European Union. It is a potent reminder of why the EU was founded on the values of respect for human dignity, human rights and liberty. Though each new generation and each new memorial will never be fully equal to it, we must continue to engage with the memory of the victims of the Holocaust if we want to prevent the recurrence of genocide in the future.

Dr James Smith is chief executive of the Aegis Trust and the UK Holocaust Centre.

The Art of Commemoration – Holocaust Memorials and their Makers

Julia Weiner

Marion Davies's excellent photographs show the array of memorials around Berlin commemorating the victims of the Holocaust. Increasingly, monuments can be found around Europe where the crimes against humanity took place and in the countries to which survivors and refugees fled.

Some are absolutely monumental, such as we see here in the cemetery-like *Memorial for the Murdered Jews of Europe*, which occupies a five-acre site in central Berlin (page 63) and has become a tourist attraction in its own right. There are also many smaller, subtler memorials commemorating specific incidents of persecution or particular victims.

Some memorials are strongly figurative, representations of people or of objects. Some are architectural, and others are completely abstract. Many of the most recent can best be described as conceptual art. In some cases, entire buildings can be viewed as Holocaust memorials, such as Daniel Libeskind's Jewish Museum (page 10). In several cases, world-famous contemporary artists have been involved in designing Holocaust memorials.

Many of the early memorials incorporated figurative elements. These can, however, be hugely problematic. First and foremost, how can any figurative work – be it painting or sculpture – even begin to convey the enormity of the crimes committed against Jews and other groups during the Nazi era and the fact that 11 million died?

Another problem is how to portray the victims. Many depictions of Jews being deported can reinforce the idea that Jews were simply like sheep being led to the slaughter. A good example is the relief on Nathan Rapaport's *Warsaw Ghetto Monument*. Inspired by the carvings on the Arch of Titus, it shows a group of Jews of all ages walking to their deaths. The figures are all slight, almost ineffectual; they stoop and look out at the viewer with huge, terrified eyes. In Vienna, the *Monument against War and Fascism* was found degrading by many Jews, including Simon Wiesenthal, who successfully campaigned for a more fitting Holocaust memorial to be built elsewhere in the city. The sculpture refers to the persecutions meted out on Jews after the *Anschluss*, when they were forced to clean the streets with scrubbing brushes. Cast in bronze, it depicts an old man crouching on the street on all fours. It again reinforces the idea of a cowering, ineffectual people and there have been problems with its being used as a seat or picnic table. However, sculptures that depict the skeletal survivors of the concentration camps can bring more dignity to their subjects, showing how humans can survive despite such adversity. One of the most moving examples must be George Segal's *The Holocaust, 1984* in Lincoln Park, San Francisco, where the one living figure who stares out over barbed wire is cast from a man who had himself survived the concentration camps.

When figurative memorials go the other way and celebrate examples of heroism, another problem arises. The results often bear a close resemblance to monuments erected by the Nazis themselves. Hitler, of course, famously detested all forms of modern art, including Expressionism and Abstractionism, and instead promoted traditional figurative artists. Similar styles were favoured by the Soviet Communists in their heroic depictions of the proletariat. The *Warsaw Ghetto Monument* also features a sculpture commemorating the Ghetto Uprising. In contrast with the dejected figures of the deportees, the ghetto fighters appear strong and full of energy, their bodies muscular and their poses reflecting a determination to resist fiercely. In Buchenwald, in a similar vein, Fritz Cremer's sculpture shows oversized prisoners armed with flags making defiant gestures as they revolt against their SS guards. The subject could easily be mistaken for a group of workers campaigning for better rights. It was made in 1958, when Buchenwald was part of the GDR and used particularly as a detention centre for anti-fascists.

Perhaps the one area in which a figurative sculpture is fitting is when it commemorates a single person. Thus when commissioning a sculpture to commemorate the Swedish diplomat Raoul Wallenberg, who saved so many Jewish lives in Budapest, it made sense to make it figurative. In 1997 a sculpture by Philip Walker was erected in London. This includes a full-length sculpture of the man but it also incorporates references to the protective passports that he issued. By contrast, the more abstract Raoul Wallenberg monument, *Hope*, in New York City, designed by Swedish sculptor Gustav Graitz, comprises a replica of Wallenberg's briefcase – five pillars of hewn black granite on one of which a sphere balances precariously – and stones which once paved the streets of the Jewish ghetto in Budapest. There may be references to Wallenberg's life story in the monument but, as a whole, the piece does not work and the London memorial offers a better insight into Wallenberg's achievements.

Despite the disadvantages of using figurative sculpture, there are indications that survivors prefer them. In 1957 Henry Moore chaired a jury to select a memorial for Auschwitz from the 426 designs submitted through open competition. The prevailing art form at the time was Abstract Expressionism and many of the designs put forward were abstract. These were admired by the artists and critics on the jury but were viewed with hostility by the survivors themselves, who complained 'we weren't tortured and our families weren't murdered in the abstract.'

Perhaps due to the taste of contemporary juries, many memorials installed in more recent years have displayed a more conceptual approach, particularly those erected in Germany and Austria. James Young has described them as 'countermonuments' – 'memorial spaces conceived to challenge the very premise of the monument' that insist that the visitor take a more active role in the act of commemoration. An example of this is Horst Hoheisel's *Aschrott-Brunnen Memorial* in Kassel. There the artist was invited to consider a way of replacing a monumental fountain that had been given to the city by a Jewish businessman in 1908 but had been destroyed by the Nazis. Hoheisel built a replica of the fountain but, after having displayed it above ground for a few weeks, he inverted it and sank it into the ground on the fountain's original location. Now, all that is left in the square are some channels of water which rush underground and an iron grate and thick glass windows through which viewers can peer down to the fountain below. As visitors stare down into the void, they take the place of a memorial above ground. A bronze inscription explains the fate of the original fountain, remnants of which have been placed around the square.

Finally, I would like to describe another Holocaust memorial in London which involves the viewer in the act of remembrance. Anish Kapoor's memorial for the Liberal Jewish Synagogue is made of black Kilkenny limestone and weighs over five tons. On the outside, the stone is craggy and scarred, bringing to mind the scars of the Holocaust that will never fade as well as crooked gravestones in Prague. Inside, it has been hollowed out to create a highly polished void. The positioning of the work is crucial. It is directly in line with the everlasting light that hangs in the synagogue and a small opening in the wall means that the light is visible from the foyer. The viewer, standing in front, is aware of an everlasting *yahrzeit* (memorial candle) in the centre of which they appear upside down. Like so much of Kapoor's work, the viewer is drawn into the void, but here becomes part of the memorial itself.

Julia Weiner is a writer, lecturer and museum educator. She has been the art critic of the *Jewish Chronicle* since 1993.

Holocaust Memorials of Berlin

Marion Davies

Walking through the streets of Berlin, you notice a large number of Holocaust memorials. They appear everywhere – on a street corner, in a market place, even on a bridge overlooking railway lines. The memorial might be a sculpture, an art installation or a brass plate set in the pavement. Now part of everyday Berlin, the memorials reveal what was a vibrant community, until its tragic demise.

Creating this work has helped me understand more about my parents' life in Germany. It has also highlighted for me German Jewry's mistaken belief that they had successfully integrated into German society prior to Hitler's rise to power.

Like many of my generation, I was reluctant to visit Germany.

From my visits, however, I derived a deeper understanding of the dilemmas Germany faces in dealing with the legacy of the Holocaust. These include acknowledging the loss of a significant part of its population and culture through the emigration and annihilation of German Jewry. I have also gained a wider knowledge of the National Socialist euthanasia programme and the persecution of other minorities.

My hope is that my photographic work will in some way contribute to confronting the dangers of discrimination and extremism.

London, April 2007

To my parents, Herbert Bier and Lieselotte Bock, who were fortunate, and to all those who did not survive and live to see their grandchildren.

Architecture as Memorial

'The theme of culture and trauma, the void, and
the experience of architecture can be talked
about in conceptual terms as well as expressed in
concrete reality.'

Daniel Libeskind [1]

Trauma

Jews have lived in Germany since the early fourth century, through eras of tolerance as well as periods of anti-Semitic violence. Following their emancipation in the eighteenth century, the Jews slowly integrated into German cultural, artistic, scientific, economic and social life. All this came to an abrupt end with the 1933 election, which brought Hitler and the National Socialists (Nazis) to power. In the six years before the Second World War, the Nazis instituted a rule of terror, persecution and murder. By the end of the war in 1945, six million European Jews had been murdered.

Daniel Libeskind's design for the Jewish Museum, shown in this photo, is deliberately unsettling. Through the building's architecture, the visitor is confronted with, and becomes part of, an exploration of the empty space left by the annihilation of German Jewry and the destruction of hundreds of years of Jewish culture.

Site: Jewish Museum, Berlin
Architect: Daniel Libeskind, 1999

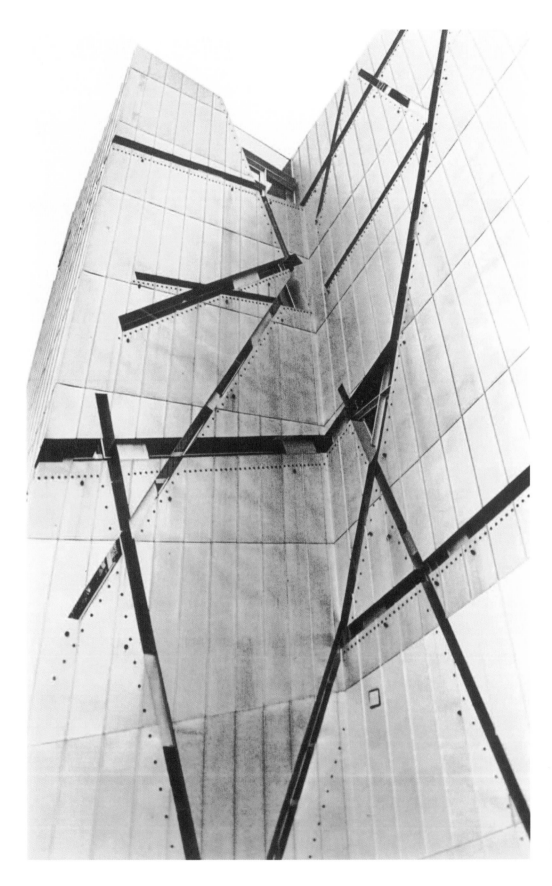

Holocaust Tower

The interior of Daniel Libeskind's building uses architectural space in a series of *Voids* – six vast, empty, concrete halls – to express the absence of Jews in Europe following the Second World War. This serves to commemorate those who were deported and murdered and acknowledges the generations that were never born.

Accessed through an underground passage, the dark, tomb-like *Void*, The *Holocaust Tower* has high, bare, cold, concrete walls sloping ever upwards towards a slit of light; normal everyday traffic noise is just audible.

Site: Jewish Museum, Berlin
Architect: Daniel Libeskind, 1999

Shalekhet – The Fallen Leaves

In this installation of 10,000 screaming, anonymous faces by Menashe Kadishman, each face could be said to represent 600 Jews murdered by the Nazis. The installation also symbolises innocent victims of war and violence.

The faces, constructed from coarsely cut, heavy iron plates, fill the entire floor of a *Void* in the Museum. Kadishman's intention is that the visitor should walk on his installation, and the resulting sound, which echoes in the bare space, is loud clanking and metallic screeching.

Site: Jewish Museum, Berlin
Artist: Menashe Kadishman, 1997–99

Garden of Exile and Emigration

Emerging from the Jewish Museum's dark corridors into Libeskind's *Garden* only provides temporary relief as it comprises 49 concrete pillars which stand on a tilted ground plate. Walking between the pillars, visitors experience the disorientation and insecurity of exile. Of Germany's 500,000 Jewish citizens in 1933, over half had fled by 1938. However, fleeing from National Socialist Germany was full of uncertainty and many, having settled in countries which were later occupied by Germany, were subsequently deported to their death.

Site: Jewish Museum, Berlin
Architect: Daniel Libeskind, 1999

Fragments of Jewish Life and Achievements Before 1933

'The prominence of German Jews and the
contributions they made became fully
apparent only after they had gone.'

Amos Elon [2]

Moses Mendelssohn: Enlightenment Philosopher

Moses Mendelssohn (1729-1786), the revered Enlightenment philosopher, is buried in the oldest Jewish cemetery in Berlin, which opened in 1672. The cemetery was full, with an estimated 3,000 graves, by 1827.

None of the graves exists today. In 1943 the Gestapo vandalised the tombstones and, using Jewish forced labour, destroyed the cemetery, throwing out the bones of the deceased. The devastation was total and only one freestanding gravestone, marking the approximate burial site of Mendelssohn, has been re-erected in the empty space. The site remains consecrated, but few realise this as they enjoy what appears to be a public park.

Site: Grosse Hamburger Strasse 26, Berlin

Oranienburger Strasse Synagogue

This synagogue, with its gilded cupola, is located at the heart of a once-vibrant centre of German-Jewish life. It opened in 1866 and was, at the time, the largest synagogue in Europe, with almost 3,000 seats. During *Kristallnacht* (The Night of Broken Glass), on 9 November 1938, the head of the local police precinct, Wilhelm Krützfeld, prevented the Gestapo from destroying the synagogue by informing them that it was an historically important and protected building.

The building was, however, damaged by Allied bombing in 1943. The front facade and entrance were retained when the damaged synagogue was demolished in 1958. Restoration began in 1988 and the building re-opened in 1995 as a memorial, museum, community centre and library.

Site: Neue Synagoge, Oranienburger Strasse 29, Berlin

Jewish Science and Scholarship

Weimar Germany after 1919 offered to Jews opportunities which had previously been available only in theory. University education was made accessible, enriching all levels of scholarship. German Jews became prominent in science, philosophy, music and culture, spheres which consequently flourished.

On 10 May 1933, less than four months after coming to power, the Nazis publicly burned the works of hundreds of Jewish, Marxist, pacifist and 'decadent' writers. Prominent sites for the bonfires were chosen in university towns across Germany. In Berlin, the burning took place in Bebelplatz, opposite Humboldt University. It is commemorated there today by Micha Ullman's *Bibliotek* memorial, located under cobblestones and protected by glass, of empty, white book shelves. This was covered by ongoing construction work during my visits to Berlin.

Max Reinhardt and Experimental Theatre

The reputation of the influential Austrian-Jewish theatre director Max Reinhardt (1873-1943) was firmly established by 1905, when he was chosen to become director of the Deutsches Theater in Berlin, Germany's most celebrated theatre at the time.

Reinhardt was committed to experimentation and was innovative in his use of lighting. He staged massive, imaginative productions and pioneered the placing of the audience within the scene. In 1919 he opened an enormous theatre, the Grosses Schauspielhaus. In 1920 he helped found the Salzburg Festival, where he annually staged *Everyman*, with the Austrian Alps as his backdrop.

After 1933 his position was under threat and, following the expropriation of his theatres, he left Germany and emigrated to America.

Site: Deutsches Theater with memorial bust of Max Reinhardt, Schumannstrasse, Berlin

Sporting Champions

This picture shows a selection of swimming medals belonging to Annemarie Pisker, who was born in Vienna in 1919 and was a 1930s Austrian National Champion freestyle swimmer and winner in 1937 of the celebrated Across All Vienna Danube race. The medals awarded to her father in the First World War are also included.

Annemarie Pisker was a member of the Hakoah-Vienna Sports Club, founded in 1909 after legislation barred Jews from Austrian sports clubs. Challenging the prevailing anti-Semitism, the club was extremely successful, at one time boasting over 5,000 members. Triumphant in football, they became Austrian national champions and famously defeated West Ham at Upton Park (5-0) in 1924.

Hakoah's women swimmers dominated the Austrian championships through the 1920s and 1930s. In 1936 Judith Deutsch was the first Hakoah member to receive an award reserved for Austria's top three athletes. Subsequently, she and two other swimmers refused to represent Austria in the 1936 Berlin Olympics, having learned that there were in German public spaces signs saying 'Jews and dogs forbidden'. Austria stripped them of their medals and disqualified them from all competitions.

Medals: Collection Annemarie Pisker

Patriotism in the First World War

More than 100,000 Jews volunteered to fight for Germany during the First World War, representing about one fifth of the Jewish population. A total of 2,000 became officers, a rank not previously open to Jews; 12,000 died in combat; and 30,000 were decorated, of whom 11,500 received the Iron Cross.

Many veterans, especially those who had been decorated, made no attempt to leave National Socialist Germany when it might still have been possible, as they believed, erroneously, that their military contribution and honours would be respected. The military gravestones are well maintained, in contrast with the rest of the cemetery, serving as recognition of Jewish soldiers' contribution to Germany.

Site: Weissensee Jewish Cemetery, military section, Berlin

Jewish Optimism during the Weimar Republic

The size of this gravestone characterises Jewish optimism in the Weimar period – a belief that Jews had at last been accepted into German society.

The last death recorded on the massive family tombstone is that of Robert Kerb, who died on 10 August 1924. The spaces were intended for following generations, but have remained empty since the annihilation of German Jewry. Weissensee, established in 1880, is the largest Jewish cemetery in Europe, with more than 115,000 graves spread over 104 acres. Most of those buried here have no direct descendants. Only 400 families, dispersed across the globe, still pay for the annual upkeep of their family graves. The deteriorating and crumbling gravestones and mausoleums are of serious concern.

Site: Weissensee Jewish Cemetery, Berlin

Germany's Largest Department Store

Jewish entrepreneurs made a significant contribution to German commerce and were instrumental in establishing large department stores. The Kaufhaus des Westens, Ka De We, was built in 1904 and remained in Jewish ownership. After the Nazis came to power, as part of the 'Aryanisation' of Jewish enterprises, the controlling Tietz family, in common with other Jewish business owners, was forced to sell out at an artificially low price.

'Picketing the Big Shops'

The Guardian, 10 March 1933
During the busiest shopping hour this evening the following scene could be witnessed outside the Kadewe [sic] ... Storm Troops marched up to the shop, formed a cordon in front of the entrance, and put up a large notice, "Germans! Don't buy from Jews". The people inside the shop left hurriedly and no others were allowed to go in. The police looked on with apparent indifference. Many people who had assembled outside seemed to be favourably impressed by this demonstration, and talked cheerfully to the Storm Troopers, who assured them that "they would put an end to the Jewish shops".

Site: Places of Terror We Must Not Be Allowed to Forget, memorial erected by League for Human Rights, 1967, Wittenbergplatz, Berlin

Regina Schrimmer Lived Here. Deported 1942. Died in Riga

German Jewry maintained a highly organised system of welfare, community, social and educational institutions. This building was used by a number of these organisations.

Since 1993 the artist Gunter Demnig has placed over 4,500 brass-plate *Stolpersteine*, (Stumblestones) in about 60 German cities, towns and villages. Each is embedded in the pavement in front of the homes of Jewish, gypsy, homosexual and political and Holocaust victims. Local inhabitants cannot therefore avoid 'remembering' the individual's fate. Members of the public, particularly school pupils, are encouraged to research their area's pre-war population, raise money for the project, and help hammer the stones into place.

The *Stolpersteine* project has established that Regina Schrimmer, born 1885, lived in the building when it was used as a hostel for homeless Jewish women and girls. Her name is enshrined on the memorial plate.

Site: *Stolpersteine* in Auguststrasse 17, Berlin
Artist: Gunter Demnig

The Exclusion of Jews from German Society After 1933

'It was an assault upon every Jew in Germany: an attempt to turn all German Jewry into an outcast, fit only for persecution, harassment and expulsion. The Jew would be driven from every profession and then from the life of the nation.'

Martin Gilbert [3]

'Jews are Prohibited from Swimming in the Wannsee Lake, 22.8.1933'

Hitler's explicit aim was to restore Germany's power in the world by destroying all political opponents and 'purifying' the German race. Jews were considered racially inferior, and their persecution and the enactment of restrictive laws began immediately on his coming to power.

The 1935 Nuremberg racial laws legitimised earlier anti-Semitic decrees by depriving Jews of German citizenship. A series of edicts followed, insidiously and relentlessly excluding Jews from German society and impacting in a devastating way on their civil rights and professional and everyday lives.

An installation, comprising 80 anti-Semitic decrees, has been hung on lampposts in the Bavarian Quarter of Berlin. In this way, local residents are regularly confronted by their district's uncomfortable past.

Site: *Places of Remembrance* memorial, Bayerischer Platz, Berlin
Artists: Renata Stih and Frieder Schnock, 1993

Jews are Forbidden to Perform the Works of Beethoven

Before the rise of National Socialism, Jews were major figures in the cultural life of the metropolis – in the arts, music, theatre and cabaret.

After the boycott of 1 April 1933, however, Jews were prohibited from performing in public. From 1934 they were forbidden to produce work by German dramatists such as Schiller or to publicly read the works of Goethe. From 1937 Jews were forbidden to perform music by Beethoven and, after Austria's annexation, by Mozart.

The memorial commemorates the popular Kulturbund Deutscher Juden (Cultural Association of German Jews). The Kulturbund provided work for Jewish performers, writers and musicians and became a place where Jews could legally attend theatre and concerts.

Site: Memorial on the site of the Kulturbund Deutscher Juden, Kommandantenstrasse 57, Berlin

Life in the Balance

Jews were particularly prominent in the art world, as academic art historians, and as commercial art and antique dealers.

After the 1935 Nuremberg Laws it was decreed that 'Jewish art and antique dealers are not allowed to practise their profession. Their businesses must be closed within four weeks.'

This permit, allowing Herbert Bier, an art dealer, to take up temporary residence abroad, was obtained in 1936 after a lengthy bureaucratic process. It was valid only until 1938.

Permit and superimposed scales: Collection Herbert Bier (father of Marion Davies)

Kristallnacht – The Destruction of Jewish Property

This entrance portal is one of the few remains of the massive Fasanenstrasse Synagogue, which survived the state-sponsored pogrom of *Kristallnacht*, The Night of Broken Glass. Between 9 and 10 November 1938, more than 2,000 synagogues in Germany and Austria, including at least 44 in Berlin, were destroyed, desecrated or closed. Jewish property across Germany, including tens of thousands of shops and homes, was also vandalised and destroyed.

In total, 91 Jews were killed and over 30,000 Jewish men between the ages of 16 and 60 were arrested and sent to Dachau, Sachsenhausen or Buchenwald concentration camps, joining Jews already imprisoned there. Conditions in the camps were terrible and the *Manchester Guardian* reported that inmates were subjected to 'great barbarities'.

Site: *Memorial Courtyard*, Jewish Community Centre, Fasanenstrasse 79-80, Berlin

Ursula Gilbert (née Brann), a *Kindertransportee*

Immediately after *Kristallnacht* the British government eased immigration restrictions for children under 17, allowing them to enter Great Britain from Germany, Austria and the occupied Czech lands in what became known as the *Kindertransport* (Children's Transports).

Quaker and other non-Jewish refugee organisations, working with the British Jewish Refugee Committee, rescued 10,000 unaccompanied children. Placed in British foster homes and hostels, most children never saw their parents and families again.

Ursula's father, Ferdinand Brann, was active as a volunteer in helping the Jewish community in Berlin. This included working in the Jewish organisation which organised children's transports. Orphans and children with parents in concentration camps, or those otherwise unable to support them, had priority. A life-saving seat on the March 1939 *Kindertransport* was found for 15-year-old Ursula, but her sister Stephanie, ten months older, was not so lucky.

The outbreak of war meant that Ursula, alone in England, could no longer be

reunited with her family. In April 1943 her parents, Stephanie and husband, whom she had married the day before, were deported to Auschwitz, where they were all murdered.

Ursula is photographed reading letters from her father. These came almost daily at the beginning of her stay in England. They continued after the war began, arriving via her uncle in neutral Sweden, detailing the deteriorating conditions of her family, until the day they were deported.

Identity Card

In 1938 Jews in Germany became obliged to carry identity cards stamped with the letter 'J' indicating their Jewish origin.

From 1 January 1939 all German-Jewish subjects were officially required to add as their second name either 'Israel' for men or 'Sarah' for women.

Identity Card of Manfred Bock (grandfather of Marion Davies)
.

The Yellow Star

Decrees compelling Jews to wear a distinctive badge on their clothes were first introduced into individual administrative districts of annexed areas of Poland during 1939. From 19 September 1941 all German Jews aged over six years were forced to sew a yellow star on their clothes. The intention was both to humiliate them and to ease segregation. It also dangerously marked them out and anyone wearing a star was liable to be imprisoned or shot. When deportations began, rounding up was facilitated.

The star was based on the *Magen David*, the Star of David, a universally recognised symbol of Jewry that can be seen on this simple memorial, located on the site of the former Jewish Home for the Elderly. From 1942 the building was used to assemble Berlin's Jews prior to deportation.

As is traditional, visitors have placed stones on the memorial to express respect and indicate that the deceased have not been forgotten.

Site: *Memorial to Deportation*, 1985, Grosse Hamburger Strasse 26, Berlin

Hiding and Praying in Weissensee Jewish Cemetery

By June 1943 approximately 5,000 Jews remained in Berlin despite the city's having officially been declared *Judenrein* (free of Jews). This figure included forced labourers, those married to Christians or of mixed birth, and a small number who went into hiding. The cramped roof of this mausoleum, where the singer Joseph Schwarz (1881-1926) was buried, provided a small space for several Jews to hide.

From 1943 the cemetery became the only Jewish place of worship in Berlin. Weekly Friday night services, attended at great risk by a dozen or so Jews, were led by Rabbi Riesenburger, who was protected by his marriage to a convert.

Site: Mausoleum of Joseph Schwartz, Weissensee Jewish Cemetery, Berlin

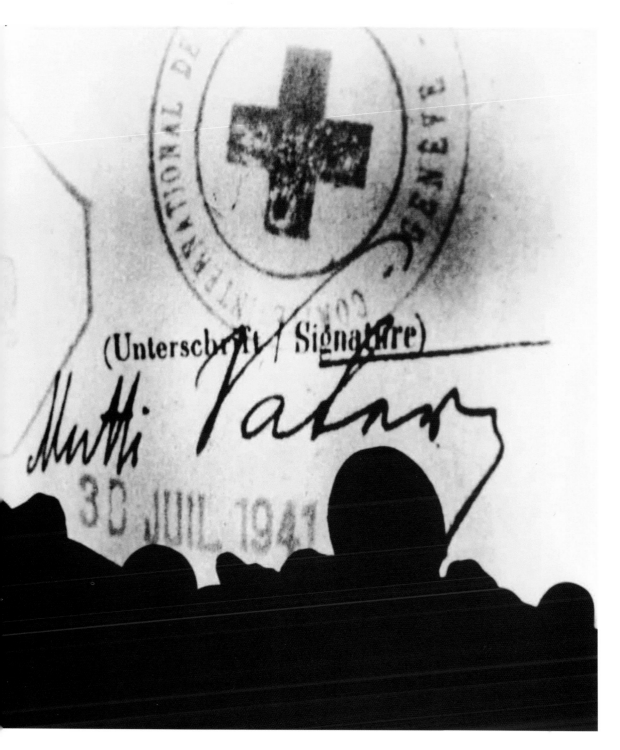

Communicating in Only 25 Words

From 1939 until 30 November 1945 the Central Prisoners of War Agency (Red Cross) sent 50,117,357 letters and telegrams and received 48,451,804. Only 25 words were allowed in their standard communications.

Liesl Glas, aged 20, managed to leave Vienna in 1939 and worked as a children's nanny for a Jewish family in Cheltenham. Her parents, despite having travel documents for America, had no visas, and all efforts to obtain them on their behalf failed. On 30 July 1941 her parents used their 25 words to write to her from Vienna:

'Much beloved. We hope you are healthy and happy with your good friends. We are too. We embrace you deeply. Love and kisses. Mummy and Daddy.'

On 15 August 1942 Liesl's parents were deported from Vienna to Izbica-Lubelska, Poland. Liesl never heard from them again.

Letter to Liesl Glas, now in the archives of the Jewish Museum, Berlin

Other Persecuted Communities Across Germany 1933-1945

No no: they definitely were
human beings: uniforms, boots.
How to explain? They were created
in the image.

I was a shade.
A different creator made me.

Dan Pagis [4]

Euthanasia

In his desire to ensure the so-called purity of the German race, Hitler ensured that early in 1933 a law was passed to forcibly sterilise those showing symptoms of mental illness or mental or physical disability. An appeals procedure existed, but most appeals were turned down. By the end of the war, over 400,000 people, young and old, had been sterilised.

In October 1939 Hitler secretly authorised the Euthanasia programme *Aktion T*. It is estimated that around 200,000 people considered socially unacceptable were murdered under the guise of 'mercy killing'. Initially, young children were given lethal injections or starved in special clinics. The mass gassing of adults living in institutions followed. They were not medically examined: their fate was determined by replies to a standard questionnaire.

In August 1941, following protests about the killings, especially from the clergy, *Aktion T* officially ceased. The killing, however, continued secretly through starvation, drugs and injections. A number of the people involved in the programme were subsequently active in establishing and operating the extermination camps.

The sculpture, in memory of those killed, is located at the site of the Chancellery, from which the programme operated.

Site: *Berlin Junction* memorial, Tiergarten Strasse 4, Berlin
Artist: Richard Serra, 1987

Homosexuals

The Nazis regarded homosexuals as 'impure' and socially deviant. From early 1933 their organisations were banned and the cafes and bars they frequented were raided or closed. In 1934 the Gestapo compiled 'pink lists' and the persecution intensified.

An estimated 50,000 homosexuals were imprisoned. Between 5,000 and 15,000 were sent to concentration camps, where many were subjected to cruel medical experiments. It is not known how many died.

This commemorative plaque, situated near the location of the raided bars and cafes, alludes to the pink triangle worn by homosexual concentration camp inmates.

Site: Nollendorf Platz, Berlin

Sinti and Roma

In 1933 there were around 30,000 German citizens who were Sinti or Roma ('Gypsies'). The Nuremberg Racial Laws of 1935 did not mention them specifically but, like Jews, they were viewed as racially inferior, classified as second-class citizens, deprived of their civil rights, and subject to arrest and detention.

The persecution intensified after the outbreak of war. They were resettled in Jewish ghettos in occupied Poland and subsequently deported to Auschwitz and other concentration camps.

An estimated 500,000 Sinti and Roma died between 1933 and 1945. The plaque in Sachsenhausen is one of the few markers in the Berlin area of their fate. A memorial near the Reichstag in Berlin is, however, being planned.

Site: Sachsenhausen concentration camp and memorial.

Black Victims and Sterilisation

There are no memorials to remind the German public about the persecution of some 20,000 black people by the Nazis, which had its origins in racial discrimination and marginalisation in Germany prior to 1933. The black population was not regarded as a major racial threat, but German racial 'purity' was ensured through sterilisation.

Between 1935 and 1937 some 385 'Rhineland Bastards' were secretly and forcibly sterilised. These were the mixed-race 1920s offspring of the occupying French colonial troops in the Rhineland after the German defeat in the First World War. The children of German colonialists and African women largely suffered the same fate.

Those who had been sterilised were eligible for the German army. Others were sent to concentration camps, where some were subjected to cruel medical experiments or brutally treated.

In the absence of a memorial, this photo with its severed branches symbolises the inability of this persecuted group to reproduce.

Jehovah's Witnesses

Jehovah's Witnesses, whose religious beliefs prevented them from swearing allegiance to Hitler and his regime, were subjected to intensive persecution. Though offered the chance of freedom if they renounced their beliefs, most refused.

Paul Gerhard Kusserow, now 75, came from a Witness family whose persecution was typical of the period. His two brothers were executed for refusing military service. In common with about 12,000 Witnesses from Germany and occupied countries, his parents and five older sisters spent between four and seven years in prison and/or concentration camps, facing maltreatment and torture. In total, almost 2,000 Jehovah's Witnesses died.

When the three school-age siblings of whom Paul Gerhard, aged eight, was the youngest, refused in school to say *'Heil Hitler'*, they were removed by two policemen and placed in a National Socialist reformatory school. Despite tough conditions in such schools and being forced to live with National Socialist families, Paul Gerhard and other Witness children (almost 800 were taken from their parents) refused to renounce their faith. Paul was separated from his family for over six years.

Deportation and Death

'There is no place in normal life for stories
which are so outrageously horrendous that
they seem like fairytales at best, and gross
exaggerations at worst.'

Anita Lasker-Wallfisch [5]

The Final Solution – Document Submitted at the Wannsee Conference, 20 January 1942

On 20 January 1942 15 high-ranking Nazi bureaucrats met at Wannsee, a suburb of Berlin, to co-ordinate the 'Final Solution of the Jewish Question' and seal the fate of 11 million European Jews. In this document, prepared for the conference by Adolf Eichmann, European Jewry was divided into those living in countries already under German occupation (A) and those not yet occupied (B).

The document shows the high priority given to the wholesale murder of Jews as Germany overran Europe. Estonia, *Estland*, had been occupied in August 1941. By January 1942 the document shows it to be *Judenfrei* – free of Jews. A total of 200,000 Jews from Lithuania, *Lettland*, did not appear on the list as they had already been systematically murdered between July and November 1941.

Document exhibited at *The Wannsee Conference House Memoria*l

L a n d		Zahl
A. Altreich		131.800
Ostmark		43.700
Ostgebiete		420.000
Generalgouvernement		2.284.000
Bialystok		400.000
Protektorat Böhmen und Mähren		74.200
Estland	– Judenfrei –	
Lettland		3.500
Litauen		34.000
Belgien		43.000
Dänemark		5.600
Frankreich / Besetztes Gebiet		165.000
Unbesetztes Gebiet		700.000
Griechenland		69.600
Niederlande		160.800
Norwegen		1.300
B. Bulgarien		48.000
England		330.000
Finnland		2.300
Irland		4.000
Italien einschl. Sardinien		58.000
Albanien		200
Kroatien		40.000
Portugal		3.000
Rumänien einschl. Bessarabien		342.000
Schweden		8.000
Schweiz		18.000
Serbien		10.000
Slowakei		88.000
Spanien		6.000
Türkei (europ. Teil)		55.500
Ungarn		742.800
UdSSR		5.000.000
Ukraine	2.994.684	
Weißrußland aus-		
schl. Bialystok	446.484	
Zusammen:	über	11.000.000

K210405

372020

The *Abandoned Room* Memorial

German Jews, and later their European counterparts in occupied countries, lived in constant fear of the sound of boots pounding up the stairs, the hammering on the door and subsequent night-time arrest by the Gestapo.

This memorial in a residential square in central Berlin, next to a children's playground, hints at the Nazi rule of terror.

Site: *Abandoned Room* memorial, Koppenplatz, Berlin
Artists: Carl Biedermann and Eva Butzmann, 1996

The Missing House Memorial

Christian Boltanski discovered that the pre-war residents of two apartment buildings, exposed after Allied bombing, had all been Jewish. He positioned plaques with their names and professions on the exposed walls of *The Missing House* memorial to indicate where they had once lived.

'Vacated' homes, following the Jewish residents' deportation, were allocated to Berliners, who generally appropriated the abandoned possessions.

Site: *The Missing House* memorial, Grosse Hamburger Strasse, Berlin
Artist: Christian Boltanski, 1990

43

The Synagogue Used as a Collecting Point Prior to Deportation

Levetzow Synagogue, built in 1914 and at the time one of the largest synagogues in Berlin, once stood on this site. In 1941 the Gestapo used it as a collection point for the deportations. Up to 1,000 Jews a night were taken from their homes, brought here and deported to the concentration camps listed on the metal memorial in the background.

Site: *Levetzow Synagogue Memorial*, Levetzowstrasse 7-8, Berlin
Artist: Peter Herbrich. Architects: Jürgen Wenzel and Theseus Bappert, 1988

Did Anyone See Them?

Situated in an exclusive, residential Berlin suburb, the freight yard of Grunewald Station, next to the passenger platforms, had regular transports to the ghettos of Theresienstadt and Riga and the concentration camps of Auschwitz and Maly Trostenets.

Fearing protests if a more central location were to be used, this suburban station was chosen for the deportations. The local villas were occupied by high-ranking Nazis, who would not be expected to object.

Site: *Grunewald Deportations Memorial,*
Grunewald Station, Berlin
Artist: Karol Broniatowski, 1991

Track 17, Grunewald Station

Between October 1941 and 1945, 35,000 Jews from Berlin were deported to the concentration camps from two stations, one at Grunewald and the other at Pulitzstrasse.

The memorial, *Track 17* details the date, number of Jews taken and the origin and destination of all transports. Even as Germany was losing the war, importance was still given to exterminating the Jews, as this photograph of a section of the memorial shows.

Site: *Track 17*, Grunewald Station, Berlin
Artists: Nikolaus Hirsch, Wolfgang Lorch, Andrea Wandel, 1998

Their Last Journey

Steps that are no longer steps, stairs that are no longer stairs; broken symbols of roads that are roads no more.

For those, who were forced on their last journey over ramps, train tracks, steps and stairs.
Translation of text on the memorial

Located below the bridge was Pulitzstrasse station, from which many Berlin Jews were deported. The memorial has been repeatedly vandalised by right-wing extremists.

Site: *Putlitzbrücke Memoria*l,
Putlitzbrücke, Berlin
Artist: Volkmar Haase, 1987

The Fate of Those Imprisoned in Theresienstadt (Terezin)

From November 1941 Theresienstadt, a former military fortress and garrison town near Prague, functioned as a ghetto, prison and transit camp for German, Czech, Austrian, Dutch, Hungarian and Polish Jews. From 1942 these Jews were regularly deported to other ghettos, concentration camps, and extermination camps in occupied Eastern Europe, where few survived.

About 90,000 detainees were transported to their deaths. In addition, about 33,000 died of starvation and disease due to overcrowding and the appalling conditions in Theresienstadt.

In contrast, the several hundred mainly elderly Danish Jews, whose government attempted to protect them, mostly survived.

Official List: Czechoslovak Relief Action: List of Persons Imprisoned in Terezin/Theresienstadt. Issued March 1945. Compiled according to official and private information received until 31st December 1944. Wiener Library, London

The Victims

This sculpture, designed by Will Lammert, was part of an unfinished memorial originally intended for the Ravensbrück concentration camp for women.

Following the artist's death, the GDR commissioned the work, dedicating it to all victims of fascism and ignoring the site's history as a Jewish home for the elderly. The home had been requisitioned in 1942 as a collection and deportation point for Berlin Jews.

Site: Grosse Hamburger Strasse 26, Berlin
Artist: Will Lammert, 1957, erected in 1985. Lammert (1892-1957) fled Germany in 1933 for the Soviet Union and returned to East Berlin in 1951

Remembering 1,723 Missing Jews

Die Spiegelwand, (The Mirrored Wall) located in the midst of the busy daily market in the Steglitz district, is engraved with the names, dates of birth and addresses of 1,723 former local residents.

Local officials and members of the public used aesthetic arguments to resist the memorial's planning stage. Underlying their opposition was the concern that the memorial would act as an unavoidable and uncomfortable reminder of a past, which many wished to ignore or forget.

Site: *Die Spiegelwand*, Hermann-Ehlers-Platz, Steglitz, Berlin
Artists: Wolfgang Göschel, Joachim von Rosenberg, Hans-Norbert Burkert, 1995

One Person Can Make a Difference

'The ultimate question for a responsible man
to ask is not how he is to extricate himself
heroically from the affair, but how the
coming generation shall continue to live.'

Dietrich Bonhoeffer [6]

Political Opposition

On becoming Chancellor on 30 January 1933, Hitler immediately ordered the arrest of opposition Reichstag deputies and thousands of left-wing activists. Most were taken to Sachsenhausen concentration camp, where conditions were severe and many died. In July 1933 all political parties, except the National Socialists, were banned, eliminating all political opposition.

This memorial commemorates the 96 members of the Chamber of Deputies; Social Democrats and Communists, who opposed the National Socialists and were murdered or died in concentration camps during the Third Reich.

Site: *Memorial to Murdered Reichstag Deputies*, Reichstag, Berlin
Artist: Dieter Appelt, 1992

Pastor Dietrich Bonhoeffer

A memorial to the theologian Dietrich Bonhoeffer (1906–45), who actively opposed the Nazi regime and its policies, stands outside the church where he was a pastor.

In general, the church hierarchies supported the Nazi regime when it came to power in 1933. The Roman Catholic Church signed a concordat, or agreement, with the new government, recognising the legitimacy of the Third Reich. The Protestant Church became united into a single Reich Church, with Hitler as its head.

In reaction, prominent pastors such as Martin Niemöller and Dietrich Bonhoeffer formed the Confessing Church, resisting the authority of the Nazi state. Bonhoeffer became one of its most radical theological voices. He was arrested in 1943 for his role in the German resistance and was hanged in Flossenbrück concentration camp in April 1945.

Site: Zionskirche, Zionskirchplatz, Berlin
Artist: Karl Biedermann

Herbert Baum

Herbert Baum (1912–42) led an anti-fascist resistance group, the German Communist League, whose membership by 1936 comprised mostly young Jews.

On 18 May 1942 more than 30 young men and women were involved in an attempt to burn down Soviet Paradise, a Nazi propaganda exhibition in Lustgarten, a vast square in central Berlin, where many Nazi rallies had been held.

The attempt failed and the members of the group were executed. Additionally, hundreds of Jews were randomly rounded up and executed or sent to concentration camps.

Site: *Herbert Baum Memorial*, Lustgarten, Unter den Linden, Berlin
Artist: Jürgen Raue, 1981

Otto Weidt

In 1941 Otto Weidt (1883-1948), a non-Jew, established a workshop in a courtyard near the Hackescher Markt to manufacture brushes and brooms. Almost blind himself, he employed Jewish forced labourers, most of whom were blind or deaf. Classifying his employees as essential war workers, Weidt prevented their deportation by bribing the Gestapo. When deportation became inevitable, he found hiding places for them and their families. Many were denounced and deported, but 27 survived.

Originally students discovered, restored and opened Weidt's workshop. It has now become a museum. Yad Vashem recognised Otto Weidt posthumously as 'Righteous Among the Nations' in 1971.

Site: Otto Weidt's Workshop for the Blind Museum, Rosenthaler Strasse 9, Berlin

The Rosenstrasse Protest

On 27 February 1943 some 4,700 men and a few women, who had previously been 'protected' by their marriages to non-Jews, together with their sons, were rounded up and detained in the former Jewish Community Welfare Office on Rosenstrasse in preparation for deportation to Auschwitz.

Around 3,000 wives, mothers, relatives and some passers-by stood defiantly outside the place of detention for more than a week and successfully demanded their release. This is the only known effective attempt at mass protest during the National Socialist period.

Site: *Block der Frauen*, Rosenstrasse 2-4, Berlin
Sculptor: Ingeborg Hunzinger, 1995

Ginette Fournier-Rouquet

Yad Vashem has recently recognised Ginette and her parents, Eva and Georges Rouquet, as 'Righteous among the Nations' for saving a French-Jewish family, the Friedmans. Ginette plays this down, saying that she 'was young'.

In 1943 the Rouquets hid the Friedmans in the attic above their shop in Villeneuve Sur Lot. Headmaster Gaston Bourgeois, who provided forged identity cards for his Jewish students, protected their son Jacques in a nearby school. He has also been awarded the honour 'Righteous among the Nations'.

Villeneuve became too dangerous. Ginette obtained false documents from the Resistance in May 1944 and took Jacques to an isolated farmhouse near Roquefort, surviving an identity inspection by the German military police en route. Jacque's parents and Ginette's husband joined them later. For weeks Roquefort cheese was their main source of food until the Liberation.

Ginette moved to London and lost touch with Jacques, although their parents remained in close contact. Jacques contacted Ginette in 2003 and they resumed their friendship, which Ginette felt was like 'rediscovering a family member'.

The Diplomats: Lutz, Wallenberg and Others

During the Second World War many thousands of Jews were saved or shielded by courageous diplomats, of whom 84 are known about. They operated at great risk to themselves in more than 18 countries in occupied Europe.

One of these diplomats was Swiss Carl Lutz (1895–1975), based in Budapest who from 1942 issued emigration permits to Jews.

After the German occupation of Hungary in March 1944 and the mass deportation of about 500,000 Jews living outside Budapest, Lutz negotiated permission to issue 'protective letters' for a further 8,000 Hungarian Jews. Not content with this, he duplicated the serial numbers of the letters several times, never exceeding the number 8,000. Additionally, he placed about 30,000 Jews in 76 'protected' houses. In total, he saved the lives of an estimated 62,000 Jews from deportation to the extermination camps.

The Swedish diplomat Raoul Wallenberg (1912-?), who is presumed to have died in Soviet custody, also used protective letters and safe houses in Budapest, thereby similarly saving tens of thousands of Jews.

During their lifetimes, few of these diplomats received recognition for their bravery and actions; many indeed were dismissed from their posts. Lutz, exceptionally, was awarded the title of 'Righteous Among the Nations' by Yad Vashem in 1965 during his lifetime.

Site: *Carl Lutz Monument*, Dob utca, Budapest

IN HONOUR OF
MAJOR FRANK FOLEY

THE SPY WHO SAVED THE LI...
OF MORE THAN 10,000 ...
FROM THE HOLOC...
BORN AT 7 WALROW ...
HIGHBRIDGE
23RD NOVEMBER ...
DIED 8TH MAY ...
RIGHTEOUS AMONG ...

The British Spy: Frank Foley

Frank Foley (1884-1958) worked in the British embassy in Berlin during the 1930s as a passport control officer. This was a cover for his work as an MI6 secret service agent.

Through these two roles, Foley obtained a clear understanding of Hitler's ruthless rise to power, the subsequent treatment of the Jews and the fate that was in store for them. A committed Christian, he recognised their desperate situation and, showing great bravery and compassion,

saved at least 10,000 lives through issuing visas, forging passports and papers and many other ruses, thus enabling Jews to escape to Britain and Palestine.

Foley, with no diplomatic immunity, did this in violation of British and German regulations, always interpreting the rules loosely and at great personal risk. Many of the thousands helped to safety with forged visas he had supplied were unaware who had saved them. Thus he was only posthumously awarded the

honour 'Righteous among the Nations' by Yad Vashem in 1999. The British embassy in Berlin unveiled a plaque in his honour in 2004; his home town of Highbridge in Somerset erected a plaque in 2000 and a statue in 2005.

Site: Plaque in the *Garden of Remembrance*, 2000, Highbridge, Somerset
Frank Foley Statue, High Street Highbridge, Somerset
Artist: Jonathan Sells, 2005

Danish Family Alsing

When the Germans occupied Denmark in April 1940, the Danes retained certain administrative powers, ensuring that no 'special action' would be taken against the Jews or any other citizens. This held until October 1943, when Hitler decided Denmark was to become *Judenrein* – free of Jews. Dr Duckwitz, a German naval attaché, leaked the plan and the Jews went into hiding, initially in private houses, churches and hospitals. Within a short period, the Danes managed to spirit more than 7,000 Jews across the water to neutral Sweden.

The stateless Bier family, who had escaped Berlin in 1933 and were now with five children aged between 14 years and six months, were hidden by the Alsings. With just a few hours' warning, the Alsings took this family, whom they had never previously met, into their home. They cared for them for ten days until passage was found to take them, in an overfilled fishing boat, to Sweden.

There are now 55 living descendants of the Bier family. Ruth Bier (70) and Lise Alsing (82) met again in London in 2006 following their brief encounter in occupied Denmark in 1943.

Epilogue

No end to night
For an extinguished people

Jacob Glatstein [7]

Memorial to the Murdered Jews of Europe

Of the six million European Jews rounded up, deported to concentration camps and murdered by the end of the Second World War, approximately 200,000 were German Jews. The 10,000 German Jews who survived owed their survival to the Rosenstrasse protest or to having been hidden by non-Jews whose actions had endangered their own and their families' lives.

This massive cemetery-like memorial, close to the symbolic Brandenburg Gate and the Reichstag, acts both as an important reminder of the past and as a hope for continuing German democracy.

Site: *Memorial to the Murdered Jews of Europe*, Ebertstrasse, Berlin
Architect: Peter Eisenman, 2005

References

1. Daniel Libeskind 'Trauma' in S. Hornstein and F. Jacobowitz (eds.), *Image and Remembrance*, Indiana University Press, 2003, 43.
2. Amos Elon, *The Pity of It All: A History of the Jews in Germany, 1743-1933*, Metropolitan Books, 2002, 9.
3. Martin Gilbert, *The Holocaust: The Jewish Tragedy*, St Edmundsbury Press, 1986, 42-3
4. Dan Pagis, 'Testimony', transl. S.Mitchell, in Hilda Schiff, (ed), *Holocaust Poetry*, St. Martin's Press, 1996, 43.
5. Anita Lasker-Wallfisch, *Inherit the Truth 1939–1945*, DLM, 1996, 13.
6. Dietrich Bonhoeffer, *Letter and Papers from Prison*, Simon and Schuster, 1997.
7. Jacob Glatstein, 'Without Jews', transl. C. Ozick, in Hilda Schiff, (ed.), *Holocaust Poetry*, St. Martin's Press, 1996, 187.

General references
Columbia Encyclopaedia, Columbia University Press.
K. Duewell, 'Jewish Cultural Centres in Germany' in *From the Enlightenment to the Second World War*, (eds.), Reinherz, and Schatzberg, Brandeis University Press, 1985

Martin Gilbert, *The Holocaust, The Jewish Tragedy*, Collins, 1986.
Martin Gilbert, *Kristallnacht*, Harper Collins, 2006.
Andreas Huyssen, 'Monument and Memory in a Postmodern Age' in *The Art Of Memory*: Holocaust Encyclopaedia, United States Holocaust Memorial Museum.
Holocaust Memorials In History. Ed: James Young, Prestel 2004.
Ingke Brodersen/Jewish Museum Berlin *'Stories of an Exhibition, Two Millennia of German Jewish History'*, Jewish Museum, Berlin, 2003.
Johanna von Koppenfels, *Jewish Cemeteries in Berlin*, Berlin Edition, 2005.
Simone Arnold Liebster. *Facing the Lion*, Grammaton Press, 2000
Steve Lipman, *The Last Rabbi of Berlin*, article in The Jewish Week, 20.04.01
Clarence Lusane, *Hitler's Black Victims*, Routledge, 2002
Bill Rebiger, *Jewish Berlin*, Jaron, 2005
A. Roth and M. Frajman, *The Goldapple Guide to Jewish Berlin*,. Goldapple, 1998.
Michael Smith, Foley, *The Spy Who Saved 10,000 Jews*, Coronet Books, 1999.

James Young, *The Texture of Memory: Holocaust Memorials and Meaning*, Yale University Press, 1993.

Resources
History archive of Jehovah's Witnesses in Germany.
Jewish Museum archives, Berlin
Wiener Library, London
Yad Vashem, The Holocaust Martyrs' and Heroes' Remembrance Authority

Internet
http://fcit.usf.edu/holocaust
http://www.yadvashem.org

Film and exhibition
Black Victims of the Nazis, exhibition, X5 Studio & Gallery, London, 2006
The Holocaust Exhibition, Imperial War Museum London,
Purple Triangles, film, director Martin Smith, Starlock Pictures, 1991
Resistance to National Socialism exhibition, German Resistance Memorial Centre
Watermarks, film, director Yaron Zilberman, Kino, 2004